WHAT FILLS YOUR HOUSE LIKE SMOKE

WHAT FILLS YOUR

E. McGREGOR

HOUSE LIKE SMOKE

Thistledown
Press

Thistledown Press Ltd.
Unit 222, 220 20th Street W
Saskatoon, SK
S7M 0W9
www.thistledownpress.com

Library and Archives Canada Cataloguing in Publication

Title: What fills your house like smoke / Erin McGregor.
Names: McGregor, Erin, author.
Description: Poems.
Identifiers: Canadiana 20230566251 | ISBN 9781771872522 (softcover)
Classification: LCC PS8625.G7357 W53 2024 | DDC c811/.6—dc23

Cover artwork: Jazz Aline
Cover and book design by Ingrid Paulson
Printed and bound in Canada

Thistledown Press gratefully acknowledges the financial assistance of The Canada
Council for the Arts, SK Arts, and the government of Canada for its publishing program.

Canada Council   Conseil des arts
for the Arts   du Canada

sk
arts

Canada   Saskatchewan

TABLE OF CONTENTS

In memory of my grandmother Dora,
whose hands were always soft when they held me.

And to the ghosts of all her secrets —
may they forgive my imagination.

Instructions for the Death of a Grandmother

Drag your hangover to the hospital and sit with your grandmother
while she is dying. Listen to her death rattle and count the lengthening
seconds of apnea the way one might count the minutes between birth
contractions. Be amazed at how long a body can go without taking a
breath. Comfort your mother who is pretending not to smell the stale
alcohol on your skin. Wonder if your grandmother can smell it.
Wonder if it is comforting or repelling to her. Keep your fingers busy
by alternating between holding your grandmother's hand and knitting
a fuzzy purple scarf for no one. Take a break and go to the cafeteria to
eat Jell-O with a dollop of fake whip cream because that's what your
grandmother would have bought you. Later, go again and eat a
surprisingly good BBQ chicken dinner. Absorb the hours and hours.
Keep counting the moments between the gurgle-thick breaths. Drink
can after can of soda pop. Keep thinking the end is imminent. Hope
for the end and feel ashamed. Absorb more hours. Watch the light
leave the window. Watch the darkness soak into the window like a
stain. Feel jittery and hollow as the night deepens. Hear the quiet
creeping through the ward. Give in to the nurses' suggestions and take
your mother to the family room down the hall. Lie down with your
mother on top of the polyester bed cover and close your eyes. Start
awake to a nurse's urgent whisper, and hurry back to your grandmother's
room. Reach for your grandmother's hand but note its cool, claw-like
texture. Slide your hand under your grandmother's blanket and lay it
on her naked stomach, be reminded of rising bread dough. Feel relieved
it is still warm, almost alive. Keep your hand there for a while. Resist
the urge to fold into/onto your grandmother's body. Be comforted by
your mother. Try to comfort your mother. Attempt to close your

grandmother's eyes and find it not at all like the movies. After several attempts, manage to get them mostly closed so that your grandmother looks like she is pretending to sleep but is watching you through the fringe of her eyelashes. Try to close your grandmother's mouth but give up when her jaw resists and your efforts tilt her whole head back. Say goodbye. Let your feet leave the hospital. Drive with your mother to your parents' house in the middle of nowhere in the middle of the night. Stop at a 24-hour gas station and let your mother buy you a Twix bar. While you wait in the car, notice the way the gas-bar lights make everything look silver. Notice the song that is playing on the radio and file it away in your memory as a signifier of this moment. Years later, forget what song it was and feel bereft. Years later, experience moments when your synapses misfire, causing you to forget, just for an instant, that any of this happened at all.

How do I write you?

I write you blurred
ephemeral, the way you show up
in dreams without
translation
from my lesion to yours

I write you on a platform
leaving
with your children who are only eyes
barely over
the window ledge

I write you with the perpetual loop
of your cadence, your reed
in my head, the sound
of your laugh, deep
throat-base, blossoming
from your lungs

I write you here in this room I've made
mine
and yours, your aprons
hanging from the bookshelf
a photograph of your mother
scowling
or maybe contemplating
all these lives tumbled
out of her

legs, the shape and seeping
river flowing, pooling, flowing

it pools here, around us
these small words

DOTTED LINES

DOTTED LINES

Portrait of Dora I

Start with an animal
something with long limbs and finely
whetted claws
a cat, perhaps? power in the muscle
grace in the gesture, yes

start there, see

how she preens
meticulous, how her affection
fickles at the first stroke against
the grain of her

coat, slick sheen and not one strand out
of place, but look closer for the small stains
blood on the bib, the flash-
show of teeth and air, a warning

do not corner her, the cut will be swift
the wound will fill
infection will redden and rise, creep
up your arm to your heart and by the time
she forgives you

returns to curl
at your lap and purr
(so deeply you might break with the ache of it)
the fever will have already
taken hold

My Grandmother's Lovers

These are the ones I know about: two Harrys and a Walter, the Widower in the Senior's Home, the Jewish Boy by the River.

Walter's real name was something else. He had been places, was a businessman, had magical money, a son from a previous marriage, a record. He gave her two babies and not a penny more.

Harry #1 was a soldier with a wife and a son, stationed at the bridge during the flood of 1950. She brought him sandwiches. He gave her a fur collar, a third baby, two divorces.

Harry #2 was her AA sponsor, ran away with her to the Shuswap, Spain, Portugal, pawned everything she owned. He gave her a plastic hospital bracelet with her name and birthdate on it.

The Widower in the Senior's Home was a glisten on her lips, then a scowl. She avoided the games room. He gave her a locked door.

The Jewish Boy by the River still softened her, six decades later. He was a secret she turned over and over like a pebble in her mouth. She gave him the sweetest smile I ever saw her give.

Taché Avenue, 1936

there was that time you and a friend went swimming
in the Red

you didn't know how, waded only to your knees,
the serpent of water shocking
and delicious on your naked
legs, the mud
sliding between your toes

the sun jumped and sparked
like tiny
white fireworks

when you looked up, your friend zipping
past, you
thought her black hair was a scarf,
caught in the current and then
gone

you never tried to swim again

Portrait of Dora II

the photographer places a chair
in front of the marbled backdrop that hangs
like a swelling wall, he gestures

she thinks of the laundry she hasn't brought in from the line
dotted now with petulant weather
she thinks
of the breakfast she couldn't eat, thinks: coffee

she sits in the chair, willing
her spine to make space, to spread the thick
of her belly up, out
thinks of her son folded
like a red note inside her

a husband, an awkward stepson shuffle
assemble around her and the chair
she thinks of leaves falling

the stepson's arms hang like dead branches, his hunched back
she thinks: daddy long legs
the husband places the weight
of a long-fingered hand on her shoulder
she thinks: maybe

On the death of my grandmother's first husband

It might have happened like this:
early morning, before the babies were up, before
all the men who filled the house
commenced
coming in and out of doors, stomping, laughing,
muscling their way into every space.

It might have been inside that holy
early hour
house still in her grip, the silence
held like a full teacup. She stokes

the stove, pours the flour
adds baking powder, softened lard, water.
She works the dough smooth and rolls it
on the table, cuts squares
and pricks each with a fork.

She is placing the bannocks on a floured baking tray
when the phone rings, rips
a jagged seam.

She raises the heavy receiver and listens.

Behind her, coffee babbles in the enamel percolator.

When she drops the tray, it clangs
and skids on the painted floor.

Dough and flour dust scatter.
A baby starts to cry from the crib.
Footsteps overlap on the stairs. The house
erupts.

Harry #1 (a portrait of my grandfather)

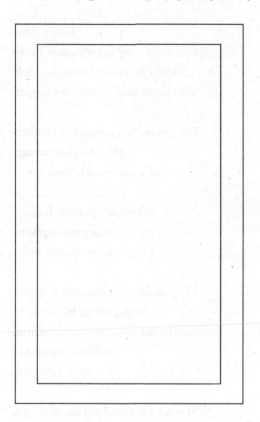

this is all that I will say
about him, for now.

Flurry thick
spring snow—my grandmother packs
her children in layers, forces their feet
into boots stuffed with newspaper.

They wrap the youngest in blankets
place her, like an egg,
on a sled used to haul wood.

Everyone's pockets bulge—
wax paper packets,
bannock and jerky.

My grandmother lingers a last look
in the mirror by the door,
strokes the fur collar on her shoulders,
a gift she ought not
have accepted.

Where are we going? cry the children.

The door opens—
the wild, wet world blows in.

She carves the snow.
The older children trudge behind.
She jerks the rope of the sled.
The egg wobbles.

Journey

They take turns pulling the youngest child in the sled.
At night, they unroll a stained oilskin tarpaulin, sleep dreamless and hungry.

The air begins to warm.
The snow is sticky, then wet.

By the time they reach the banks of the North Saskatchewan, the sled drags
on mud and rock.
The river is high and swift.
They stop.

Give me your clothes, the mother says.
The two older children slip behind a thin screen of dogwood.

The youngest wriggles free on the naked bank, pushes pink toes into mud.

The mother gathers up all the clothes, heavy and ripe with days of walking.
She ties each garment to an old cottonwood until the tree looks full of
other people's prayers.

What do we wear now? ask the older children.
The youngest watches them, places a handful of mud inside her mouth.

Metamorphosis

Spongey with matted grass pierced
by saplings, the bank
is steep. Heat
from the midday sun releases
a cloud of musk: sedge,
vetch, sticky
yellow poplar.

She rips up handfuls
of old foxtail and cattail, twists
green willow branches until they yield.

She sits on a rock by the river and begins to weave,
weaves all day
and into the evening. New skins
for her naked children.

At last, when the wet chill of spring dusk clings
to her aching fingers, makes
the children shiver and cry,
she finishes.

Put these on, she says.
They put on the things their mother made for them,
step out of the thin bushes
and into the dimming light.
Good enough, she says.

Then she slips from her own skin—and steps
gingerly into the black river.

She stands in the frigid
water, night glinting
around her ankles.
She stands in the water.

The children grow weary of watching their mother.
The children, warmed by their new clothes, grow sleepy.
They fall asleep to the sound of the river
and the sound of the river glinting
around their mother's ankles.

Edmonton I

Edmonton starts out slow: a boarding house
with faded clapboard, crumbs of night-raided garden
clinging
to their shoes. Contraband carrots.

Edmonton is a thin soup, at first.

But he is industrious and perhaps
this is why she sleeps beside his viscous dreams.

He hates them all but
wants them, too.
His want is an always-empty pot.

They drive an old station wagon to every small town,
delivering cases of potato chips. She
does the books, handles the phone. The soup
thickens.

Soon the clapboard boarding house is theirs.
Soon a sprawling bungalow.
Soon the jewelry, soon the fur, soon the top shelf.

They dine at dress-code restaurants
where he retrieves her from toilet-stall floors
and carries her, like a hunter with his kill,
to the cold car.

Edmonton II

Her children are   trying to kill her   don't they understand how
to stay out of the way   the gaze of men   the hands of men
unseen   insistent   will always find an opening

theragetheragetheragetheragetheragetheragetheragetheragetheragetherage
the   rage
the range
the rain
their age

her hands, her aching eyes, her empty
mouth

everything is under water because
she holds it down

I don't know the half of it

but maybe this: maybe
Harry #2 was handsome
undoubtedly charming (when did she ever take to an uncharming man?)
and when she stepped, tentative, beat, all Birks gold and coiffed hair
into whatever church basement he had been lurking
she was cooked
and he was hungry.

Maybe it was audacity
or maybe courage,
the steeling to flee one life
for another, to pack up and drive away with a new lover, a dream,
a suitcase full of divorce
money, no forwarding address—or maybe it was none of that,
just cowardice and easy foolishness.

And maybe when she got out of the hospital
after Harry #2 beat her up and cleaned her out,
stole her dogs,
maybe all the wind was knocked from her sails
as she sat in the backseat of a taxi

ride from Salmon Arm to the place
she thought she could build by the water,
and all that was left were the bones of a dream,
a package of saltines and a case of Happy Pop

maybe that was enough to
keep her
afloat until the next thing.

A Dog Named Popcorn

Somewhere inside the illusion of the life she wanted, out by the glinting water with her new man, my grandmother bought two toy poodles—white balls of fluff—that barked and peed on the rugs. She called one Popcorn, the other Butter. While she was on an all-inclusive solo trip to the hospital, her lover packed up everything she owned and skipped town in her new truck. All that remained of Popcorn and Butter were a couple of damp rugs on the floor. She never saw her lover again, but one day she did see her truck in the parking lot of BiWay Foods. Inside the truck was Popcorn, peeing on the bench seat. She stole back her dog, and she and Popcorn lived a quiet existence, out by the water, until my grandfather broke yet another marriage to be with her. And he loved that dog, got him to stop peeing on the rugs, took Popcorn everywhere. Years later, when my grandparents moved to a place where dogs weren't allowed, my Uncle took Popcorn in. When Popcorn died, my grandparents were staying with us and my Uncle called with the news. It was the first time I saw my grandfather cry. My grandfather—hunter, misanthropic rogue—wept like a baby for the dog my grandmother's lover had tried to steal. No one ever found out what happened to Butter.

A Photograph of my Grandmother, August 1972

she is sitting in someone's kitchen
the table cluttered with stubby brown
bottles, glasses half-full, almost
empty
pastel packs of cigarettes,
an ashtray

behind her a window beckons
the green, green, long afternoon

the table is cluttered
like the beach at English Bay, low tide

she is centre frame, the room assembled
around her
noisy, active, faces turned
to the camera, a recent joke
lingering

she looks down
taps the ash from her cigarette

the orb of the flash in the window glass
hovers
like a moon over her head

she is tap, tap, tapping the ash from her cigarette
a delicate suspension

just before the salty tide of us
her children
her children's children
the wave
swells, lifts
and sucks her back

The Long End

She slipped in and out for weeks, months, once, when I arrived at her bed, she asked what day it was. October 16, I told her. Her eyes widened like a stain spreading. She slipped away again, came back, couldn't find the word for "light," kept telling me to "turn the door," moved her eyes to the naked wall and slipped away again. Stayed away a long time. Came back and told us she wanted to go home, slipped away again. No more words but her eyes would return, sometimes, groping the air until they landed on a familiar face, mine or my mother's, until they didn't.

What was it like inside there? All that time crashing into itself.

Lines

Before my mother, there was the boy
who died inside my grandmother
when she fell down the stairs, she had been carrying
a basket of laundry.

Before the boy who died inside my grandmother,
there was my baby aunt, and before
my baby aunt there was my baby uncle.
There was also

their bootlegger father, dead
in a hotel room,
six weeks shy of his thirty-sixth birthday.

And my grandmother's thirteen-year-old stepson
who ran feral, grew claws and tail and fang until captured
as a Ward of the State, disappeared
into the endless bosom of Children's Services.

Before the feral stepson and the babies and the dead husband,
there were the brothers:
the one who grew no larger than a dog,
the one who burst his appendix at twenty-six,
the ones who loved her fiercely.
The brothers in jail.
The brothers in the newspaper.
The brothers on the roof, surrounded by police.

The school friend swept away by the Red
while my grandmother watched.

The forbidden boy by the river whose name she kept
tucked under her tongue for sixty-two years.

The bottle in her father's hand. The scorn in her mother's face.
The hungry looks that followed her
everywhere. The stain
of her name.

Later, after my mother but before me, the cancer
that took her only sister and then her father
in the same month.

The streets of Toronto that swallowed one brother, the train
wheels in the Fraser Valley that bisected
another. The sea of alcohol
that could not be swum.

The darkness of marriage.
The wrath of motherhood.
The deepness of the cage.
The deepness of the cage.

HARDLINES

Because the Night

the morning   I had an abortion
she came with me   into the room
not   at first but
when it mattered   when

the poster of fluffy   white
kittens taped to   the ceiling over the place
where legs are   spread and things
scraped out   was too ridiculous to be borne alone

10,000 Maniacs doing   Patti Smith
filtered down   from the piped-in radio
and there was a   moment of

focus

hovering around   quiet nurses
the doctor   and the kittens

but the nicotine stains   on her fingers
are really all   I care to remember
of the cells   I once carried but left
in a stainless steel tray

that went where?

now, too late to take it   back
I don't wonder   what might have transmitted

through that meagre puddle   of blood and clot
I know

it was a gallant gesture   to sever
the too-familiar fear   before fixation could root
like a stubborn weed   in thin soil

Bears

There are bears in my head
muscling the deadfall
pushing hot teeth into my ear
breathing fierce
undecipherable codes of fear, they swarm
a slow approach, sideways circling.

The bears in my head claw
at the beehive under the barn's red siding
the boards wrench from their fastenings
unleashing a gush
of small bodies
vibrating, humming, furious.

I am not afraid of bees
but the bears in my head
want to kill me.

Tiny Uglies

I.

I think about his big hand, skin loose and spotted, a Band-Aid between
thumb and index finger where his grip slipped staking tomatoes, bled
all over the garden. I think about his big hand on her flat chest, the movement
of his fingers a quiet rasping on the cotton of her
shirt. I could hear it, I can still hear it. The quiet rasping
of his hand on her chest.

II.

We were once outraged at the small armies of ants swarming the baby birds
blown from their nests, pinkish ribcages fluttering, wings translucent
and raw. I once watched a platoon of ants attack a writhing earthworm surfaced
from the wet grass. Other ants gorging
on the sticky orb of a fish's eye.

III.

Years later, we discovered hands on the backs of our heads, the calm but
persistent pressure down, the momentary resistance eroded
by fear of being impolite, hurt feelings. The hands
on the backs of our heads, holding firm to the cave of damp musk. The close
humidity of cock and crevice.

IV.

I don't think I ever spoke of the pink blanket at the vet clinic,
draping her glossy form moments after
the cry of pain, stopped sudden, glide of the needle, eyes like wet marbles
uncomprehending. Her silken form on the table, hair and canine muscle, still
warm. The endless ache of the needle slip. My heart stays
there, writhing, safe from hands.

it is both things we learn at once

the coming into focus of girls like K, neat, fresh, expert at the subtleties
of facial powders and creams by age thirteen

    (is also the sharpening of us, angular, awkward, hair and clothes plagued
    by string, born with that telltale shroud, un-concealable, a warning);

we learn the clean, thick carpets of K's hallways, walls a gallery of equidistant
normalcy, framed, as if to say: *we have mastered; all beasts herein be caged*

    (becomes the threadbare surprise of our own, the things kept from spilling);

and contrariwise, one morning, we see the bandage on K's pink wrist, the deep shado~
seeping beneath

    (take refuge in the sureness of our worn and shabby life).

Saying Yes and No

I.

You knew he wasn't right when he asked for your fingernail clippings.
You hid the envelope in your jacket pocket, mailed it
from the red post box near your high school. A love letter in keratin.

While your parents were out, you called him,
asked what he was planning to do with all the little pieces snipped
from yourself. He said
he was going to eat them. And he did.

Two years later, you took three buses and a train to the psychiatric hospital
on the coldest day of the year. Sinuses cracked and bled.
He burned a teardrop into his cheek with a bent paperclip and a lighter.
He said his mother would collect his things from the apartment,
if you could just pack
everything up.

II.

You were friendly to the tuba-playing busker with the topknot and bad teeth
the way you were friendly with all the buskers in the neighbourhood.
The first time he asked you out, you smiled but said you were busy.
The second time, you were a little high
and thought, why not? It's just ice cream and a walk.

He asked if he could leave his tuba at your place. You didn't want
to be rude.
After the ice cream you told him
you had plans with friends. Told him
to get his tuba because you wouldn't be home later.
He lingered at your doorway, casting a limp net.
You feigned being in a rush, hurried off
to the bar alone.

When you got home it was late
and you were drunk.
He was waiting on your doorstep.

III.

He was ugly and almost twice your age.
He was your boss and married and you had met his wife and children.
You felt bad about the children.

You told yourself all kinds of stories to make it not matter, pretended
that the first time he took you home was a drunken hallucination.
Tried not to think about how he pulled your skirt up
and your pantyhose down
while you gripped the edge of the cold toilet bowl, eyes watering, choking up
everything he paid for.

In the months afterward, pretended
you knew what you were doing. Pretended
that each time you folded yourself into his car, idling
like a snake in some narrow alley,
you were in control. Cleaned your apartment
obsessively. Drank
so often and so much that you had to buy a special floor mat
to put beside your bed, one with a rubber backing
so that when you rolled over in the night to become
empty, the acid from your stomach
wouldn't wreck the hardwood.

Arrhythmia

after Natalie Diaz's "The Red Blues"

There is a ghost moth behind my sternum
one wing torn, fluttering blind, dusting
my ribs with talc
fingering for a slit in the screen
to let the night in.

There is an acid jazz band behind my sternum
riffing on the riffing on the riffing
getting lost, quickening, ascending
wasp-mad and careening
tripping down
the come down.

There is a junked-up punk behind my sternum
eyes half-lidded, smashing
dishes against the wall, against the floor
kicking cupboard doors to crack and
splinter, mad-laughing, muscle-coiled loud
and roaring.

There is a crowded kitchen behind my sternum
congesting the chambers, making heat
filling my lungs with smoke and grease, bad teeth
chipped porcelain, blackened pots, straw brooms worn to nubs
impractical valises, crochet doilies, sweat-shaped hats
half-empty bottles, jokes
in languages I cannot decipher.

I remember almost nothing

only: the furious-fogged oversized glasses of Mrs. M
who pinned me at recess against the school's brick wall
to deliver the shame I deserved
for my filthy mouth, my filth
in front of everyone, the shame.

only: the refuge in plastic ponies, the smooth
mysteries of other girls' pink-
carpeted bedrooms, their pink arms and cheeks, the pink
smoothness I could only imitate, feebly, until
my grimy angles revealed, they fled
to cleaner pastures, ponytails swishing.

No wonder I insisted
on learning the language of boys
scraping my knees, climbing every tree, breaking
my nose, twice
in the school yard for the closeness of boys:
chubby T with the perpetual sinus infection
who invited me to swim in his pool
red-headed R whose mother died and who cried when I fell
from the tire swing in his yard
brown M with a stutter
who laughed until he peed
and taught me the dirtiest jokes, shameless,
shameless.

when i say / love i don't
define the variety / that is spineless
or the type / that heats or
even the nonspecific / sort that gets
pitched around at / persons we don't
even recognize like / some category of
totalizing cuddle when / i say i
love you i / mean i exist
hiding behind the / door with my
chloroform rag and / this roll of
duct tape i / love you when
you are unmoving / cannot slip from
me i love / you so considerably
i will not / shift my eyes
from your hands / i love you
the way i / loved the baby
kittens i carried / around in my
pockets until they / stank and leaked
because it matters / not the damage
or the dishonesties / you fail to
guard i disregard / because i comprehend
necessity to love / you like this
is the only / syntax i recognize

The Basement

One of the married men, not
the one you seduced but the other, the one
you crashed into
after the engine fire of adolescence
so much smoke in all your
openings you didn't even feel

the altitude drop
until you were all the way down
in the basement
naked, arms
above your head, wrist-bound and
swinging you couldn't get the image of meat-
hooks from your

thighs, he held a black
riding crop, identical to one you remember using
on a stubborn palomino, now long dead
now dog food
probably, he held a black riding crop and raised
his eyes like a smoke, rising, raised

the black tip of a leather riding
crop to your skin
and you thought, too late, of going home
of riding horses, of the good smell
of dogs and dry ditches
but instead you nodded, just once
said
"do it."

things to do when you're drunk alone:

turn it up. everything. crank it all.
flail and jump around the living room, but not too much.

watch *Goodfellas, Casino, Titanic*. drink rye.
get lonely. get restless. eat leftover KD. drive

your sedan to the local joint on a Tuesday night, drink
silently at the barren bar, just one. maybe two.

miss the driveway on the way home, skid the wheels
on the gravel and when you put it

in reverse, see the hump of a dead deer on the shoulder, glowing
in the red of your tail lights.

record dispatches to yourself, your future
self or the one that's vanished. listen.

The Man with One and a Half Testicles

My cat is jealous of my long hair, keeps trying to
eat it. Remember the man with one and a half testicles? She
asks, gnawing on a braid. Yes, I say, but you don't, your grandmother's
teats weren't even full yet. Stop

trying to distract me. Tell me the story
anyway, she says. I unhook her claws from my throat. The man with one
        and a half testicles
started out as a boy with two testicles. The boy with two
testicles fell straight down a flight of stairs, landed on a foosball table, lost an
even ¼ of his perceived manhood. The boy with one and a half testicles got caught
smoking behind the grocery store, played doctor and

lost in fifth grade, grew
into the man with one and a half testicles, acquired a fondness for muted
kaftans and thick sweaters, smoked loose tobacco, drank cheap Sake, played
        doctor with
errant teenagers and won, associated with Cuban conspiracy theorists,
        fed neighbourhood cats

sardines from his basement apartment window, died from a
massive stroke
at sixty-three. No, says the cat,
licking my temple, not
like that. The man with one and a half testicles

deftly rolls a joint with nicotine-stained fingers. Passes it to the sixteen-
year-old in a park where the grass is cut and sweating. The grass is cut and sweating,

itching the backs of the sixteen-year-old's thighs, leaving criss/cross\marks,
    making her skin
nervous like ants are marching, burrowing into the milk fat that will never fully
grow to muscle. The man with one and half testicles hands the fat cocoon of
    the lit joint to the
sixteen-year-old with ants burrowing into her thighs. She opens wide, swallows
    it whole.

swimming birds and fish, a comparison of anatomy

she nearly died in the channel, wedged
between bones of dread
and agony until, with her bruised
little head, she cleaved
our mother's breakwater

I'd like to think this first violence
inured her to the rest
but that isn't how it goes; baby
skin too soft
takes years to cure

she ripped so that later I slipped
like a fish
and swam the straits she made
following her through broken
locks, she taught me

the secret reprieve of imagination
how to endure
the rage that comes
and comes

until she rose from the slick
and went

perhaps that first, great
escape

from the cage of our mother's hips
imprinted her soft skull
gave her the power

to fly far
nest elsewhere
hatch her own babies from delicate shells
so as not to bruise them
with her body

My disease had the drinking (a ditty, a round)

drinking the drinking the drinking disease
aunts drinking uncles drinking grandmother grandfather
drinking the drinking

and the drinking

first lover second lover third lover
fourth lover fifth lover sixth lover

and the drinking.

Sometimes I think I have the drinking disease
it makes me shake in the morning

And when it doesn't
when I send it away
it doesn't go far
it stays

close enough that I can watch it make
my lover shake
in the morning.

Rachel Yehuda Says

inter   mission
    gener   trans
       ational   tivity
          of epigenetic stress   cep
                                           re

        is akin to giving
        a seven-year-old a switchblade, a gift
        that keeps on taking
        but might one day save their life
        if
(for example)
        they ever need to run into a forest
        to hide from murderous soldiers.

     Then, maybe,
     they could use their shiny new switchblade
            to dig
                roots, maybe
                              kill
                              gut
                              skin
                              a rabbit

                              a soldier.

(I'm paraphrasing here.)

(Me, I have learned
to keep my switchblade folded
safe in my pocket. I know
how the warmth of my body has transferred
to its smooth metal. I like
how it feels, bent in on itself, dull. I like that
inside its inertia there is a razor
that can swivel, slice, sever.

I might need it one day
but probably not.

I sleep with it under my pillow
its blade
skinning my dreams.)

Advice to my seventeen-year-old self

It's already too late to change the way your mother made you feel, too much,
or the way shame is a thin blade you hide under your tongue, or the boy

                              who left you unaided and famished
                              on that wind-scoured farm, the length
                              of a whole hard winter
                              and then came back to knock you
                              off his skinny horse, but

don't be defined by feeling beaten up or down, you will learn the freedom of
buying your own food, which is the same thing as joy, don't waste it

                              on theatrics, don't complain
                              and cry in front of men you want
                              to sleep with, they will sleep with you anyway
                              but will not remove their clothes, rather

try to laugh among men you want to share a tuna sandwich with on a park
bench, try to remember that every man was once a boy, and

                              above all else, see everything through
                              barefaced hunger, no one
                              is watching but me, I
                              will feed you

This is not

this
thin lip, hard brow, these

children who do not approach
these men who do

this is not
who I am, knotted

with rules, logistics of dishes, grocery lists, how
everyone's shoes must line up

at the door, this
is not who I am, no one

knows except the cat and the dog
who understand the comfort of a cage

daily, we plot our escape
but fall asleep at the allotted hour, bellies full

the strained sounds of television
poisoning us slowly

even as our dreams
stay wild

a suspended paw above the loam

an ear cocked to the snow

our bodies rise from the carpet and down
shedding stupor

we are running to the wet river bank
we are running

BLURRED LINES

On Dissipation

O, my species
dilute as wind

at night we slink
into the nests of swans, hold
our breath and pray not to be
detected in the dim

glint of stars, to last
for morning cloaked
in the scent of strangers

but who doesn't hunger
to be seen? The way the blackest
hour hungers for a pulse
of light to break it

we occupy the meanwhile
hidden, hiding, holding
inside old skins of other animals, yet
searching all along
for a kind

I have yet to meet
a kin in these borderlands
that are neither shore nor
body

even the rivers know
each other, are banked

but we, dear orphans
know only the mire's ripple-
broken reflections

AGLC, 1982

brown brick means grown-ups
and legs pinched in the baby-seat cold
metal of the shopping cart shocking good in summer heat
brown brick brown bottles green bottles bare milk-
fat thighs pinched in the cold metal of shopping cart good
blue bottles brown bottles gold bottles
clinkclinkclink go bottles bare thighs in cart smooth
wheels up and down the shiny aisles of bottles
brown brick means grown-ups and grandma's brown
hands warm pushing cold metal shopping cart
good in heat of summer smooth up
and down the aisles of shining bottles

Cimetière de Saint-Boniface

Winnipeg in winter. Winnipeg   up to your knees   stripping over stones that
mark the ones   you want where?   waits and doesn't.   The stones
weather and whither the line's   wither there you   find what you want but
don't they   don't care weren't waiting   for you these stones   laying lines.

Winnipeg whither in   winter stones weigh   the lines lay you down.   Winnipeg i
winter   has weight. It pushes   your weak-kneed   withering want deeper
down. Stones   tripping up to your weak   knees laying your whether   lines.
The ones   you want lither lay   in weather wait   but don't.

Winnipeg in weathers   the lither   lines lay stones   while you want and wait
and want   and wait and want and wait   withering whether   the ones
you want don't   wait stones don't   dither   lay weather. Whither
the ones   you want tripping   stones lay wither   don't wait.

Inheritance

Avoidance, the art of skirting
his cane or his hand,
we speed like wolf
spiders, hunting in dark corners
games out
of sight, smothering giggles
erupting like
spring grass fires
that might catch wind
and burn him
up.

clean work

my grandmother may have been
a mean drunk

but Goddamn

the woman knew work
taught my mother
so that they both could shame me
while I half-heartedly smeared windows
with a flaccid rag

my grandmother left school at fourteen
scrubbing other people's floors
so she could buy herself
a garnet ring

my mother schlepped me to a rich woman's home
to be babysat by cable television
(Rocket Robin Hood, Hercules, Spiderman)
while she vacuumed deep-pile carpets

there is no shame in hard work
they assured me
from their poison cloud of Pine-Sol
and Comet cleaning powder

no shame at all

Learning to Count

twelve

you are admitted into the realm of adult knowledge. it feels violent and
unwanted. you resent your mother for giving it to you but once the gate is
opened she gives it all. an initiation. as if you are ready. words that give
shape to the shame that fills your house like smoke. before you had the
words the smoke was just the air. now you know something is burning.

eleven

your mother and your sister are sharing secrets. they lock themselves in
the bathroom and speak quietly together. you are not allowed in. your
sister has started bleeding and drifts away from you. she shaves her legs
and armpits. when you ask to have her old training bra, she and your mother
laugh. mock you. make fun of your tiny body.

ten

your grandmother makes banana cream pies. takes you shopping and buys
you whatever you want. sleeps over on the hide-a-bed and her cigarette
burns a hole in the yellow blanket. when you are at her apartment, you and
your sister still pull out the chest of toys in your grandmother's bedroom
closet, the same ones you have played with since you were a baby. only now
you don't play with them so much as examine them. artifacts.

nine

you get a gold fish for your birthday. when it dies, you sob but your
grandmother shrugs and says *easy come easy go.* she has that same look on
her face as your mother gets when you have annoyed her. your father consoles
you, pulls you to his chest to shield you from the sharpness of women.

eight

at school a teacher with an Irish accent and big horse teeth talks about the rebellion. you are excited to tell the class that your uncles fought with Louis Riel. the teacher tells you to stop telling lies.

seven

Mrs. Roberts wears black lipstick and leather skirts and you love her. but she is only your teacher in the mornings. the afternoons are a woman in a cardigan and oversized glasses who says you talk too much and are lazy. you have two friends and one of them pinches you and puts tacks on your seat. the other one only plays with you when the mean one says it's okay.

six

there is a girl who takes off her panties when she gets to school so that the boys can see her bare bum when they lift up her skirt. her mother is dead and her father packs her a lunch of boiled wieners in a thermos. you are her friend for a while and play with pictures of Smurfs cut out of a magazine in the library. neither of you has the right toys.

five

you play the Kleenex game. she places the tissue over her face and puffs her cheeks, blows it into the air. you snatch it up. demand it be done again. and again. a cigarette burns itself out in the ashtray. grandma hands are always soft and smell good. your mother is coming to collect you but there is still time for iced tea.

four

getting distracted in the supermarket. a box of cereal with a rainbow on
it. run to catch up with and reach for the polyester legs. look up and your
mother's face is alien, a stranger looking down in surprise. terror seizes
you like a tiger.

three

you love your Monchhichi monkey's plastic face and hands. soft dark
body. squint against the sun on the back step. hold your Monchhichi tight.
summer but you are velour and ruffles. the shimmery brown car waits.

two

your nose is running. someone holds their cigarette in the air over your
head, leans down while you stretch up. lips meet. perfume and tobacco.

one

she dotes. you are her Christmas pudding. the bundle of you passed freely
from one set of hands to another.

in the room with my dead grandmother

it was only an event inside that small room
nowhere else, no ripple

no one but the two of us
to witness

her eyes would not stay closed
even after we pushed the lids down
twice

the cooling
of her skin

a nurse removing tubes and needles
the whisper of her uniform
soft and light

a moth against the window

Winnipeg

sneers with bad
teeth, its incessant breathing

you know somewhere deep
throbbing in your chromosomes

an old injury, claims you
then leaves you washed up

fetid banks
the Assiniboine

pick your way home
through goose shit and shadows

all night you listen to the city
coughing phlegm-heavy down Portage

you listen to the night, the wind in those dying oaks
the loosening of time

listen and listen
waiting for your name

Lineage

good half / breeding is as natural as breathing   no need to be so loud
about it   the signifiers

are obvious to those in the know   no need
for paper pulpits / proof of pedigree   get a t-shirt

made   Marie begot Marie begot Marie Alphonsine
begot grandmother begot mother / begot me

Grant halved Falcon halved Nolin / halved Desjarlais halved Ducharme
had Lee / held ransom   have me

but what if it isn't good? / what   if   breathing   is   like   ballroom   dancing
necessitating a re-memorizing / a re-searchifying

what if the only inherited halving is left / right
shown / hidden   this hand / then that

raised / and lowered   wound / released
this tender raging   tending rage

finding of fault / lines in the whiteness   of mind

goddamn dogs

Grandma slammed / her finger in the gate because the goddamn dogs rushed / past her legs
the hinge / bent / the hinge bent her ring / a storm brewed
on her face sudden-ly I saw her / in there startling / starting to feel / fear her but I wanted
to defend the dogs   who had only been excited to see us.

Grandma slammed / grandma slammed because / the goddamn dogs / rushed her legs
slamming / goddamn dogs / grandma's finger in the gate / the hinge / I wanted
to defend / her sudden face / bent / a storm there / starting to feel / startling to fear I saw her
but I wanted   the goddamn dogs   excited / to see us.

Chimera

dit moi combien je devrais
demander, baffled in this skin
this plunged
laang
la bouche est partagée
between bitter and balm, chews
and chews its own thick meat
what else to do? la bouche est partagée
mishowayitay, cut
into strips, la laang
partagée, tastes all over
namooya ataynikaatew
blind as a mole

/

tell me how much I should
demand, baffled in this skin
this plunged
tongue
the mouth is split
between bitter and balm, chews
and chews its own thick meat
what else to do? the mouth is torn
all over, cut
into strips, the tongue
divided, tastes all over
unmixed
blind as a mole

She came thundering

into my dream
I had been looking for her
in small spaces: behind cupboard doors,
in her mother's teacups

she came thundering
behind the wheel of a big, thundering truck
young, in sepia
her children small there beside her

and yet I
was not a stranger
when she stepped from the cab
stood on the muddy planks

she spoke to me
but could not say a thing

the dead must be dead

I curled like a cutworm
around the airless space
where she had been

Zygote

You were once
a zygote.

Before that,   around like
you were split in   the even halves
two, carried   of an apple.

And   you were
          even before
                                      halved
something
          of you   in
                    existed

the germ   that would
                              cells

one
          day   become

          seed   egg

In this way you were always
deep inside

your grand/
mothers/
mother/
father
allatthesametime.

Portrait of Dora III

Hands soft as a baby bird's throat
but strong enough to lift an enamel casserole dish
leaden from the oven—rice pudding or a whole turkey
the bent middle finger
always at an angle, calling in the eye

I could not see the elegant crook of that finger
without knowing the wood splinter
that raised itself to her
pierced deep
while she was on her knees

or the man's knife that chased the splinter
severed the tendon

the white family who paid
the house with its Wedgwood set
the polished floors she soaped and rubbed
the board that split
the hands that laid it
the blade that planed it
the shoulders and the axe

the tree with its branches that the wind
once brushed
like a lover brushing the beloved's
long, black hair

Weeds

Don't judge me too harshly
for not understanding the small things
that come with your blood
this whole world is filled with white

people talking, I can't help
but be one
even though I'm trying
they have me by the roots
it's confusing having so many

seeds penetrate my skull
as if my brain was a fertile pot

but then I suppose something in me ought
to be; my womb
dried up and unused like an ornamental crab-
apple

or maybe more kin
to last year's missed potato
discovered in the garden while making space
for new
and here I've failed you twice
this shriveled potato-womb, this colonized
brain, invasive
with wrong ideas, missed understandings, groping
in the loam for what you
planted
pushing my seed deeper, deeper.

a visit

the old woman is sitting in her chair   hair coiffed and clean one long gracile leg
tucked underneath her   the door is propped open a few inches   an invitation
to the visitor who is   expected   the visitor enters   *hellooo*   and takes
off her shoes at the threshold   the smell in the small apartment is warm and
sweet   Japanese chicken wings and rice   a kiss on the impossibly smooth
and soft cheek   a coming in and settling on the chair that was once a
grandfather's   now dead   and secretly thank goodness for that

small talk

the strained   finding of things to give words to   even though both yearn
for something closer   the visitor too large now to fit in the old woman's lap
too old for the Kleenex game   the old woman   barricaded   and the smell
in the small apartment gets warmer and sweeter until   she decides   by some
mystical clock in her head   that lunch is ready

a slow flurry of activity   as if underwater she sets the table and brings the food
the visitor offers to help but   *no no you sit here*   and then   they eat
the visitor is effusive with praise   the food is so good and the old woman
smiles   delicately licks a fingertip   *yes, I've always liked this recipe*

Ghost Hunter

Still, I am never not
looking under coffee pots and floor mats, between sheafs
of old paper

never not sucking on found fragments
like salt candy.

Now I am driving to the Shuswap
sucking up the night
with a mouth full of canker sores.

Ghost hunter, I'm sniffing her out.

Maybe this road is the one she drove
with her lover and her dreams, maybe these black hills
whirring by.

Maybe this is the post office
where she licked eight-cent stamps.

Or maybe this is the path she walked
to the water she never swam
but cast stubby amber bottles into:
grocery lists, receipts, a recipe for a better life
tucked inside
and sealed
with the rubber from her shoes.

Bodies

This body wipes green goop from the soft belly of the mother's mother's body who is taking three months to die in a thin bed. The green goop comes from a clear plastic tube that burrows itself into an angry hole in the soft belly. The beautiful, long fingers of the mother's mother's body reach for this body's hands, reach for the plastic tube, paw, tug on it. More green goop bubbles out. This body looks at the mother's mother's face, tries to read the instructions. Green goop gets under the beautiful, long fingernails and stays there for days.

This body orbits the mother's body, the mother's mother's body. A schedule is made for shifts at the hospital. This body feels the pull of guilt if a day goes by without warming the space beside the mother's mother's body's thin bed. This body dreams of forgotten pets, left to starve and then rot in some closed off room. This body thinks of questions it will never ask, questions the mother's mother's body can no longer answer. This body wonders at all the secrets slowly dissolving inside. This body looks and looks in the mirror but doesn't see any bodies inside its own.

During the nights, free from the hospital, this body poisons itself so that not-good men will be liberated to express their desire for it. Not-good men grab at it, prod it, squeeze it. A not-good hand slips up this body's skirt at a party, in front of not-good eyes that see and not-good mouths that laugh. This poisoned body sits on not-good laps, considers not-good options.

One morning the phone rings too early. A grey, moist, late November morning. This body has a bad hangover that will only tolerate Diet Coke and small packets of saltine crackers until mid-afternoon. The nurses say it could be soon or it could be hours. This body absorbs a new vocabulary: Death Apnea, new, viscid sounds from the mother's mother's lungs. Yarn and knitting needles keep this body's hands busy. The mother's breaking face. The mother's mother's jagged breath. This body's reeking, poisoned sweat. Three bodies in a small room. Waiting.

This body sits in a chair next to a thin bed and respires poison for fourteen hours while the mother's mother's body takes the time to die. This disoriented body. This body belonging to the mother's mother's body dying in the thin bed for fourteen hours and also to the paler, slowly deflating mother's body as it watches. All fires extinguished. Three bodies, reluctant nodes of the same organism, waiting as one.

Notes and Acknowledgements

Acknowledgements to Susan Musgrave and Bronwen Tate in whose exceptional classes these poems sprouted. Thanks to Billy-Ray Belcourt and Keith Maillard for their astute feedback and kind encouragement on the first version of the manuscript. Gratitude to Elizabeth Philips and Thistledown Press for having faith in the project, and to Anne Simpson for her gentle and skillful editorial work.

I would also like to acknowledge the various literary journals in which several of these poems were first published: "swimming birds and fish, a comparison of anatomy" appeared in *White Wall Review*; "How do I write you?" appeared in *Room*; "AGLC, 1982" in *filling Station*; "how i was taught" in CV2; and "Weeds" appeared as "Dilution" in *Prairie Fire*.

A very special shout-out to the Friday Night Writers Café lovelies for their comradery, commiseration, and laughter: Robyn Braun, Kimberley Orton, Jason Emde, Tonya Lailey, Barbara Bruhin Kenney, Theresa Fuller, Alison Newell, Lisa Moore, Chelsea Peters, Melinda Scully, and Leslie Palleson.

I would not have written this book without the support and encouragement of Natasha Nunn, Michael Lithgow, Carissa Halton, and Darryl Bereziuk.

PHOTO BY ALEX POCH-GOLDIN

E. McGregor is a Euro-Settler/Métis writer currently living in Winnipeg, Manitoba. Her poetry, fiction, and creative non-fiction have appeared in numerous magazines including *Room*, *The Dalhousie Review*, CV2, *The Fiddlehead*, and others. She obtained a Master of Fine Arts in Creative Writing from the University of British Columbia in 2022. *What Fills Your House Like Smoke* is her first poetry collection.